ALL LOVE,

NEW AND SELECTED
POEMS

I0107841

ALL LOVE,

NEW AND SELECTED POEMS

By Diane Marquart Moore

Border Press
PO Box 3124
Sewanee, Tennessee 37375
www.borderpressbooks.com
borderpress@gmail.com

ISBN: 978-0-9997804-3-5

Library of Congress Control Number: 201896227

Cover photograph of glass work entitled *Lotus* by Karen
Bourque.

Cover design by Martin W. Romero

Printed in the United States

FOR VICKIE

ALSO BY DIANE MARQUART MOORE

POETRY
Destinations: New and Selected Poems
Let the Trees Answer
Spring's Kiss
Above the Prairie
Sifting Red Dirt
A Slow Moving Stream
Street Sketches
Corner of Birch Street
Strand of Beads
A Lonely Grandmother
Between Plants and Humans
Night Offices
Departures
In a Convent Garden
Mystical Forest
Everything is Blue
Post Cards From Diddy Wah Diddy
Alchemy
Old Ridges
Rising Water
The Holy Present and Farda
Grandma's Good War
Afternoons in Oaxaca (Las Poesias)
The Book of Uncommon Poetry
Counterpoint
Your Chin Doesn't Want to Marry
Soaring
More Crows
Just Passing Through
Moment Seized

YOUNG ADULTS
Martin and the Last Tribe
Martin Finds His Totem

Flood on the Rio Teche
Sophie's Sojourn in Persia
Kajun Kween
Martin's Quest

ADULT FICTION
Redeemed by Blood
Silence Never Betrays
Chant of Death with Isabel Anders
Goat Man Murder
The Maine Event
Nothing for Free

CHILDREN
The Beast Beelzebufo
The Cajun Express

NON-FICTION
Porch Posts with Janet Faulk-Gonzales
Iran: In A Persian Market
Their Adventurous Will
Live Oak Gardens
Treasures of Avery Island

"The best and most beautiful things in the world cannot be seen or even touched. They must be felt with the heart."
— Helen Keller —

Table Of Contents

NEW POEMS

"ALL LOVE,"

he often closes his message,
the words, a presentiment of devotion
like a short Psalm, opening chords
of a song called Enclosure.
Simply there, always known,
extending to infinity.

MUSIC

"Anything anyone says is your voice." Rumi

Grace note, cymbal crash,
silence heavy with hidden riffs;
the wren builds a messy nest
beneath our eaves,
singing lyrics without a score.

Above the hemlock
a fierce sun courts laughter,
my body eloping
with grace note, cymbal crash
into the allure of your voice,
subliminal, supplicating.

BEDROOMS

I know why Van Gogh painted
the world of his bedroom,
a single wooden bed
spread with red blanket,
pictures clinging to the wall
tipped to the angle of his mind.
He seemed comfortable
with two chairs, one for him,
another, perhaps for his brother;
no mirror needed
for untrimmed red beard.
His blue jacket hung on a peg,
part of crude trappings,
simplicity at cost… but he was safe
from the madness,
waiting for sunlight
and a good day to paint.

In my own bedroom a table
holds a book of poetry,
bright orange cover
lying atop a black Bible,
phantoms of parable and poem
vying for a place in my life;
on my walls, angels looking longingly
at a patch of blackberries,
The Dixie Flyer rushing
toward mountain peaks
across the way,
a blue and white framed mirror
reflecting sleepless nights

under a green comforter, safe,
waiting for sunlight
and a good day to write.

HEREAFTER

The "also world" of Sister Elizabeth,
not an addition,
remains the commonwealth
of here and now;

in this place venial gods and goddesses
have no supernatural power,
the trees I love
bow to winds that threaten
earth settling to its gravity;

yet nothing speaks of alternate worlds
only atoms adjusted, transformed
here and there
without going away…forever.

TWIN GREAT GRANDDAUGHTERS, LILLIAN AND KATE,

their inchoate language a babble
understood only by each other,
solitariness unknown, unwanted;

the joining of inner dispositions,
down to the last breath,
an articulation of love.

"WHEN I HAVE FEARS THAT I MAY CEASE TO BE"

Did I really request that my ashes
be entombed in a steel drawer last year?
a box that could never contain this life
of suffering and sometime rejoicing where
there is no attempt to put it back together,
after death, the resurrection not infusing ashes,
the brain that housed all my language
and longing for immortality?

Today, I went down the mountain into the valley
where an Amish woman with rough hands
sold me four ears of corn and flowers,
food and beauty that I love,
told me I seemed to be
"a good little lady,"
and my friend went into paroxysms
of haughty laughter,

threatened to buy me a tiny bonnet
made of feed sack cotton
so I could impress strangers
with my disposition to please everyone,
"become an Amish/Anglican
capable of forgiveness," she mocked,
"just a good little lady
who could carve that epitaph on a tombstone

if you hadn't requested that you be burned to ash."

II. "WHEN I HAVE FEARS THAT I MAY CEASE TO BE"

Now, if. my mentor,
former poet laureate of Louisiana,
can be a Buddhist/Catholic,
I can be an Amish/Anglican in tiny bonnet,
prone to bouts of meditation
in our dual religious beliefs;
mine, sometimes more active —
plowing fields, making jelly.
cultivating acres of corn and soy

while he meditates, plants ornamentals,
and writes poetry on sweaty walks,
is allowed running water
in which to bathe his daily devotions
without censor, and I am penalized
for taking two baths a day
invite grave censorship
from my Amish affiliation.
Still we both agree

humans need and deserve
our intense compassion,
we are apt to exhibit more tolerance
than judgment, as we forgive
trespasses seventy times over.
Today, I am encouraging my mentor
to shave his beautiful, curly gray hair,
to buy an orange robe
and present himself down in the valley
as God's good little man

"who knows the way …
things are."*

*Buddhist definition of enlightenment

THE BLUE PERIOD

I have looked at this watercolor
fifteen years sprinkling rain

on Orange Beach, Alabama,
two beach umbrellas appearing as

blue palms waving at the bluest sky,
an embankment of golden sand

near Walter Anderson's eternal Gulf
and him discovering a poet for company.

In the amateur sketch, I see a rare time
relaxing in the arms of a coast not bothered

by insolent storms, hurricanes
alphabetical and gender arranged.

Water, wind, golden sand
absent here on the mountain,

a plateau with no place to peer over,
the sun hiding in dense woods,

dark thoughts falling from a gray sky,
flash of lightning and thunder rumbling;

but I keep looking at the crude watercolor
watching for gulls to wheel overhead,

the gentle sway of bright blue umbrellas...
seen through dark glasses.

I. BROTHER'S PAINTINGS

Your shadow sits on a dwarf pier,
"I pishing," you told our mother.
just as you also said, "poot salad,"
and would that you had never learned
the letter "f" in later life,
a potty mouth you always had.

That day you disappeared to water,
you were three, already a stray
preaching wanderlust 50 years
until you landed in jail. No lakes, no woods,
only the inner staircase of dream
painting your climb in a lucent sky.

You always loved the world of water,
marooned in a hell flaming
in the hole you rendered well in art.
Only the trees spoke of home,
as you, one of the imprudent birds,
slowly moved upward and West.

II. BROTHER'S PAINTINGS

Those huge boulders you painted
in the middle of the Pacific,

miniature houses at seaside —
Crescent City, California.

Always the gulls hovering
above cold surf you loved,

the sky bluer than the mood of your life,
your wife burying your ashes on a hill

beneath a giant pine at Big Bear
because, she said, your father made his place

beneath such a cheerful form —
somewhere else but it was calm and familiar.

You keep circling the boulders
and the miniature seaside village,

lifting off with soaring gulls,
wishing she had respected your art,

would remember how you loved the ocean's curve,
green stone, enough to mark your lonely grave.

AVOIDANCE

I am also guilty of recoiling
from mawkish stories:
the pain of abused children,
dogs, deer, horses, birds,
adults, all those who suffer
in reality and memory
from having been abused
in mind, body, and spirit.
I write this knowing no one
wants to be reminded
of the fact that we humans
inflict our own brand of pain
that calls for constant correction
despite bias, ancestry,
born into, breeding, geography
and right to happiness.
And God forbid that we tell
all to others beyond the couch
of psychiatrist, psychologist or priest,
our latest languaging
of man's inhumanity to man
explained away in the catch phrase
"it is what it is"
despite indications that
"it" works better in confession
and admission than avoidance
of the universal truth with which
a friend ends his messages:
All Love.

AMONG THE MISGUIDED

I used to call her "Wattababy Yell"
never weaned, always crying for her mother
but I had to teach her dental hygiene,
and what a little make-up would do;

lectured her about her ten-year old obesity,
"If you stay fat, no one will like you."
so she absorbed the lesson, became anorexic,
every dime spent on fashionable clothes;

black boots, jodphurs, gold belts
implanted breasts spilling
out of slut-cut blouses
that finally caught a wounded man,

an Afghanistan veteran without honor,
jobless, divorced, two children,
convinced her they should marry
but live apart for a year?

She, believing the moon had risen
over Lake Tahoe and her life,
discovered he was not Disney World,
returned to the scene of Wattababy Yell —

a room filled with fashionable outfits,
the damaged electrical outlet
of her infantile fantasies, keening love
within the familiar perimeter of Self.

I. ETC.

These years of etc.
I wait for the best to happen

when I cross the boundary
between twilight and dark.

Leaning a bit to the left
in spinal rage, I deny a cane,

instead, reciting prayers for my daughters.
I listen for their voices

telling me of simple pleasures,
rapture in their tragic lives;

one, occupied with two raccoons
who visit daily: "Two Ears"

and wounded "One and a Half Ears"
feeding brazenly on dry cat food.

Through the glass of the den window
my daughter asks, "Why do you visit me?"

They do not answer but confirm the grace
for a life confined by illness,

three times a day grazing in her backyard,
and she tells me her job is to feed

impoverished creatures of the world,
like St. Francis haloed in the sunlight

keeps the sight of them in her dreams,
every morning, a coming attraction…

II. ETC.

At age 52, Elizabeth became a nurse
working Labor and Delivery,
was asked to resign because of her age,
not having legs swift enough
to appease arrogant nurses, surgeons
trying to carry bed loads of sorrow.

A cloud floated away in clear skies,
time unfolded and she fled
to peace in the backyard of California foothills
where a Mama Quail and her babies
foraged for berries and beetles,
nesting near large gray rocks

and hiding in shrubs along the shelf
of Elizabeth's abandoned dreams.
Elizabeth, at seven, whose short legs
almost missed departing school buses,
had been deemed too slow to bring infants
into a world of people impatient

to turn the page, human speedometers
unlike the slow walk of her beloved quail
who seemed to wish her well.
Elizabeth, sent home to ponder injustice,
the welcome pace of backyard creatures…
and an early sunset.

HUCKLEBERRY FINN

Memory made scant riches
for little brother, Harold Jr.,
dying in his 50's, carrying a pocket
of stones most of his life
except for one adventure
on his short journey going home.

I read Huckleberry Finn aloud to him
curled in a bedroom in which my father
had cut a hole in the roof to house
the pipe to a pot-bellied stove,
Circa 1954, nostalgia for heat
to which he had never warmed.

Memory makes riches of Harold Jr.
laughing aloud at the antics
of Duke and Dauphin,
laughter inspiring a trip
on which he and Billy Boy Reese
embarked in a stolen boat

launched on the Bogue Chitto River,
aka the Mississippi River for Harold Jr.
and his runaway friend,
overnight banked near spooky woods
before discovered by local police
curious to know why they had run away.

Was it the thought of escaping
dysfunctional families, the idea
of laughter lying beyond horizons of abuse?
or was it the freedom we all felt
making rich memories on the gypsy trip

to California inspired by our drunken father?

Harold Jr., at two years, crossing the desert
as the car fumed West,
windmills turning on small farms,
our mother pointing them out to him,
his head swiveling to catch the landscape
and saying, "Ooh gone."

I watch a documentary about Mark Twain,
see Harold Jr. paddling into an inlet
under an ancient oak tree,
thinking about putting on a show
with Billy Boy, and my memory becomes rich
with the vision of him bent with laughter

not only on the river
but standing in the front seat
of a blue Ford coupe
passing windmills and looking back,
crying out, "ooh gone, ooh gone"…
Yes, little brother, *ooh gone*.

WATCHING THE WRENS

Where have they gone?
infant wrens, directionless,
fluttering into a blue ocean,
their mother pushing, telling them
to expect warm welcomes from the unseen.

The nest now an untidy hanging,
twigs, leaves, declarations of love
twisting in the wind
beneath green painted eaves,
secure and shadowy.

Them thinking how good it was
to be fed, making noises
to call someone home,
hoping nothing would change
if they opened their beaks

and received the message:
soon, she will let you go,
and you must let her go,
singing as if you knew
where you were going.

VAGABOND

I should have known
the time would come
for vagabondage to surface
from long burial in my psyche:
the Diddy Wah Diddy trip —
Texas, Arizona,
New Mexico, California —
when my father
sold family possessions,
resigned his job
as a draftsman
and middle-class society
declaring our family
would gypsy forever
but only lasting
the summer of 1946.
What was he looking for?
clarity?
a place of agreement
past the earthbound?
a summer night
all rain and release?
For me, never forgotten,
buried beneath Respectability
Duty, Marriage, Children,
memory erupting
in my 70's after
at least twelve
of my own migrations.
This ancestral passion
for moving about,
destinations unknown,
fueled the first Marquarts

moving from Virginia
to Indiana, Ohio,
Wisconsin, Iowa,
my great grandfather
discovering Louisiana
between time out in 1897
for the ultimate adventure;
a journey by way
of White Horse Pass
to hunt gold
in a stampede,
climbing 2800 feet
to Yukon Territory
where 3000 horses
had died along a trail
later dubbed
Dead Horse Trail,
a clue he ignored.
After encountering
a 200-inch snow
packed white,
looking as if
it would stay awhile
in minus 80-degree chill,
he turned back,
gold be damned,
went home and bought
more habitable land
until he owned
the entire town
of Lake Arthur, Louisiana.
Never wanting
to vagabond again,
left his wandering spirit
bridge for other beginnings,
a legacy for my father
who passed his wanderlust
for California to two

of my male siblings
and I, the female offspring
went as far afield
as Persia,
my father's voice
echoing behind me:
"The moving finger
writes and having writ
moves on..."*

* *The Rubaiyat of Omar Kayyam*

CANTICLE TO SAINT FRANCIS

He was never vanquished,
struggling against a faithless world,
his life given sudden joy
for bathing lepers after being told:
"repair my falling house."
He moved stones from fields
overgrown and unyielding
to repair Santa Maria degli Angeli:
only a metaphor for lifting stones
from hardened hearts,

the hidden terror of helpless lepers.
He has not been stranded in history.
What garden does not hold
some replica of him
preaching to the birds,
the face of God in stone
sworn to a new life of artless piety,
allowing bees to land on
his tonsured head,
feet anchored in flowers,

immobile but holding up
an unwashed universe
to the mercy of God?
Dirty, sacred altar linens he holds
in his hands, his most gracious hands
washing them, laughing and leaping
with his brothers on the road
toward Paradise, blazing
with the light of sun and moon,
the canticle of rebirth.

THE VALLEY

We go down to the valley,
familiar place of corn and soy,
dandelions curling around seasons,
no happenings in the slow pace
of lives well-lived.

I like it better than the mountain,
rocks overhanging this placidity.
the way down is easy,
shadows merging in woods
along the curving road.

I imagine the valley people
never having known
anywhere else except the way home,
late summer light leading them
toward the village of Cowan;

trains still thundering through
but limestone quarries long closed,
the Texaco gas station now a museum.
We pass through the town silently
and when we return

at the far edge of town
Angus cattle have come out
to take their stand out of sun's heat,
bunched together under a tree
where crows flap, caw misfortune.

I feel the loss of place
going up the mountain again,
light fading gray,

phantoms overtaking us
as we ascend the stone walls beyond…

I. DAUGHTER

Midnight in Ochsner's
I am not there
and will not be
to give you a kiss
before they shuttle
you away to count backward
into darkness again;

A mother praying
hundreds of miles away
for your body to rise
and know health,
no longer burdened with Self
but known to love
however imperfect.

Change from a deep center
that once knew the sun,
singing "rump pa pa pum,
rump pa pa pum,"
little drummer girl dancing
in a red velvet dress,
days turning back

to missing you and
found wrapping a rubber rat,
in a bath towel,
"Appley Dappley," you said,
tending something smaller.
You innocent and beloved,
contrary but safe.

This moment I sit
waiting at the window
watching Squirrel Nutkin
at play, leaping for you
and I send you all love
bound to this uncut cord,
arms outstretched.

II. DAUGHTER

After the surgery I go looking
for a colony of saints to thank
for her coming through;
this morning in early light
both of us grounded in safety

despite my nightmare
of driving a new car
too close to a cliff
then pulling back
in time to save a passenger;

despite the drawn curtains
hoping to see her appear,
holding hands with someone
in a blood-stained gown
walking over a long bridge;

surprised at how agony
and tenderness
resemble one another.

LOTUS

The Sisters of St. Mary say
Sister Mary Zita wanted to cut
and eat a flower yesterday
while she sang in *Igorot*
to the spirits of the dead.

Hospice workers claim Sister
has nine lives and fights against
leaving her sock cap with white stars
to anyone else who could pull
the sky out of it any time.

She wishes to take the cap with her
to the Holy City
or to her old address in the Philippines
and some days she howls in the halls
of the Convent, the Sisters waiting

to run up the mourning flag any time.
But I'm waiting for her to arrange
one more bouquet for the altar
instead of trying to eat petals
and leaves in the shadow of St. Mary

overhanging a corner of the chapel,
want her to cross the border
during canticles of Morning Prayer
and open the gate for a lotus
growing somewhere else.

AUNT KATHRYN

Last night, a beloved aunt
came out of darkness to visit.
She had lived during the era
when aunts often stepped in
because mothers died or failed
at care for their offspring.

The only photo I have of her
is one where she lay, legs stretched out
on her father's side lawn; a dog,
my brother, and me vying
for her attention while she posed as
a southern beauty sunning herself.

In the summers of my childhood,
I was sent to her for week-long visits
assuming life in a cottage my father
designed to hold her loneliness
and a taciturn husband who
thought more of remolding wrecked cars

than caring for her. She was, for him,
the maker of a plate of butterbeans
and cornbread every noon,
after which he would stretch out on a bed
so I could slather mentholated ointment
on his forehead for his sinus headaches.

Aunt K. was dutiful and silent,
as lonely as my grandmother
who lived up the same street —
Tenth Avenue — and when bored
I could visit her, if brazen enough

to traverse the sidewalk

near a cow at pasture
but I was chicken-hearted
and ran into the street
to get past what I had been told
was the "friendly cow,
all red and white,"

I did not love "with all my heart."*

And then, Uncle Tony died,
a suitor came to Aunt K's door
and she was lonely no more.
Mr. Passman took her on a church trip
where she was chastised by a Baptist pastor
for dancing on the deck of a cruise ship.

For the longest time, my Aunt Eleanor
called herself my godmother
although my baptismal certificate
plainly bore Aunt K.'s signature,
and I wondered why Aunt K. had allowed
her sister to assume this position.

But when my father lay abed
hooked to a ventilator
and had drawn his last breath,
I looked up and found her
at my side, standing in stead
for my dead mother, my other aunt.

My Aunt Eleanor was nowhere near;
it was Aunt K who encircled
me with the arm of a caring godmother,
saying, "He wanted to live for you children,"
and a good image entered my mind
that he had so abused in his drunkenness;

the image of him carrying me in his arms
down Third Street in Baton Rouge
because I had injured myself
in a bathtub fall… him holding
me tight against the weight of injury,
the face of love co-inhered in *hers*.

A Child's Garden of Verses, Robert Louis Stevenson

IN A FIELD OF BATTERED WEED

On my desk, a bookmark
bearing the picture of thistle,
forty years of lavender amid thorns,
a wild plant we bagged together

in a forgotten field that spring day,
unmindful of the cautionary tale
about it being an ancient symbol
of both pain and pleasure.

II. SELECTED POEMS FROM
AFTERNOONS IN OAXACA

MEMENTO

Memory, suspended,
sleeps in the pink hall
of afternoon, finally free.
We are cautioned to make arrivals
while fastened in the moment,
even as shoeshine boys nod
in the square, marimbas quiet
at last, soldiers' black boots
marched off.

Only the twenty-nine churches,
gold-tipped restorations,
loom in the stone of power unbroken,
forcing memories of time watches,
the Zapotecs waving plumes
of the national pastime: death
in the pink hall of afternoon,
the scent of gardenias
lingering on the wind.

NECKLACE

Not afraid of siestas here
we lie down, unknown
but not lost,
silent as cracked plaster walls,
undisturbed by rain and thunder rolls.

A small girl with long black braids
walks up and down
offering happiness beads:
amber, coral, pearl,
and we buy them to please her.

She encircles my neck,
fastening the clasp,
dirty face in long dress
and ragged petticoat
making my breath catch,
loosening suspended memory.

THREAT OF RAIN

Black pigeons on the cafe rooftop
watch the men in black aprons
who, smelling the rain, fold up
yellow and green plaid tablecloths;
The wind rumbles and Mickey Mouse
passes, bobbing a yellow smile...
they are taking in the balloons.

SABBATH

Sunday morning and bells are silent,
Nada, sound muffled on the *Zocalo*.
A watch lies on the bedstead
stopped at four a.m.
The narrow cobbled street
runs up to the mountain's feet,
deserted except for a white dog
shaking his long tail on the rooftop.
Mexico is yet asleep,
the blue shoeshine packages
still tied up, waiters moving slowly,
changing the tablecloths to yellow.

WE ARE ALL BEGGARS

sending postcards every day.
We keep track or boast impressions?
In the post office and everywhere
they use adding machine tapes,
increasing the cost;

We drop pesos into small baskets,
feeling the bright-eyed children's hopes,
how they mirror the poverty
but their smiles are happy flashes.

They seek to,
but do not have to buy us.
We scatter the silver like rain
from a rooftop into unfolding hands.

AWAKENING

The *Nahua* know about faces and heart
physical and non-physical;
the non-physical we make,
ixtli in *yollotl*,
face and heart making;
carry these true selves created here
where the mountains lie in shadow
where we keep trying to sleep
and awaken to a new language.
On the bureau, roses, dark as blood
droop in the white light of annunciation.

FRIENDSHIP BRACELET

A red and white woven band
she tied around my wrist
gifting me, but it was her tiny voice,
a harmony of *ixtli* in *yollotl*,
and small as the morning finches,
that made the true gift.

A miniature Zapotecan,
she sold so easily
the ware of her true purpose:
weaving.
And I said "tell her I love her voice,
it resonates with prophecy."

ALPHA

The awareness of my despair
collides with the liveliness of Mexico
happening beneath my window
in the *Zocalo* where trucks load
and unload wild animal carvings,
creations of a will to transcend
poverty and malice
or manifestations of true selves?

Slowly, the heaviness lifts,
a sparrow poises on topmost branch
of the giant ficus tree,
a schizophrenic man stretches headlong
at the door of the green stone cathedral,
butting his head on prayers of the living.

A brown-legged dwarf
carrying a colony of odd-shaped balloons
moves her short legs across cobblestone,
and, amazed, I wait
as hundreds of orange and yellow Christs
break loose, rise in the mild air.

MEXICAN MONSTER

They bought me an *alebrijes* monster,
bug-eyed, dagger in its sides,
snake-tongued Zapotec fiend
to represent the self annihilation
I practice to kill off the creative self,
a monster that eats my poems and my life.

It is a pantheistic dream in cobalt blue,
yellow, red, lurid colors,
forms of confusion,
disturbances of soul
that rise in the cloudless Oaxaca sky,
the white light I cannot bear.

CHRIST'S VENDOR

Candi Lopez, child necklace dealer,
brought in an armload of new strands,

Jesus on a black string.
"*Nada, Nada*, I have a cross, I said,

fingering the finely wrought Celtic one
but she pulled me into the hotel lobby,

held Jesus on a black string to white light
streaming through the open door to the square,

one brown eye closed, the other focused
on a tiny glass peephole in the crucifix.

"*Mira, mira*," she said, twirling around,
knowing she had caught me again.

Inside the peephole, a paper image
of Christo Rey who takes away,

who takes away all the sins in the world
and, too, my pesos at the rate of 20 a day

via Candi Lopez, head of *Zocalo* sales...
queen of international necklace dealers.

ADIOS, OAXACA CITY

Every night is Saturday night in the *Zocalo*,
hot marimba on the keys, rumba in the street,
voices murmuring on the wind.

We leave their celebrations,
orange and yellow blossoms on sandstone,
but the sun will not age before we return

lonely for the bruised stone,
wind blowing white curtains
through open casement windows

where we seek the birds of myth,
gold and black butterflies,
blue and yellow tapestry of memory

our spirits' refreshment again.
Quetzalcoatl anointing his new companions.

SHOESHINE

The sound of monkeys squeaking
is only the last shiny touch on black shoes
forcing patent gloss in a best foot forward.

We thought birds were conversing
across treetops in early morning air
or it was the preternatural sound

of the Zapotec's fantastical creatures,
voices shimmering on the air,
floating above clacking shop doors

being drawn upward,
a pleasing vision
like stepping out of old skin.

EVERYDAY JOURNAL IV.

ART WORK

Don't measure me for a frame,
I haven't completed the landscape.

I may paint over a long stretch
of old canvas with red radiance

setting fire to a psyche
the color of dark journeys.

BESIDE THE GLASS PORCH,

old friends, elephant ears,
their upturned faces

sanctify loss;
green surfaces

veined with wisdom,
curious and seeking,

wide mouths smiling.

They come to us straight
from the sacred heart of soil

entrusted with silent messages,
beguiled by mist and sun;

lift up their long necks thankfully,
content to be the way they are,

drinking in the summer rain.

ST. MARY'S PIPE ORGAN

Twelve pipes, mouths open
and Bishop cones on their heads

praise our broken world,
canticles above the table,

pure notes harmonizing
in the sweet air of piety.

This simple life caught
in the mouths of silver pipes

for the sister who sings soprano
to mockingbirds outside the glass.

Twelve pipes, holy and wakeful,
fair angels of grace notes

trebling praise in the chapel.
Thank you, thank you for infinite song.

DOGGEREL ABOUT THESE POETS

Other poets think
other poets
are not poets
because of other forms;

Other poets think
other poets
do not follow
prescribed norms;

Unrhymed verse always circumspect,
freedom of lines inciting no respect,
subject to literary anemia
if not a member of academia;

I point to Bukowski's success
as a matter of free verse digress
published: 45 books
and it looks

as though other poets might
heed his words
if other poets
really wish to be heard.

SEPTEMBER

Rain on The Mountain
is often like blood on snow;
the sight of broken branches
black with watery deaths.
Eaves drip against white stucco
to which snails cling,
afraid of the fallen sky.

Stony ground drinks noisily,
screen of mist and weight
of air also taking us under water,
a torrent that blows
leaves away like broken promises,
the weather siren
sounding in the distance.

CHRISTIAN SCIENCE

Doubt is planted in some DNA,
Divine Mind meeting the needs
of only a select few who trust
nothing is as it seems to be;
without fear of pain and discord
they sit on the lap of eternity

favored offspring of God,
the select argue against themselves
looking deep into the eyes
of a rescue sentry
who always reassures them
of chronic good fortune;

who take on the life of the unknown
and irresistible power
impervious to reason
whose spirit envelops them
in the law of love without body —
invisible, metaphysical fact;

But, if we are in his image,
heaven birds pulling down shades
against illness and pain,
why lies the seed of negativity
in some DNA, a divided mind
scarred and sorrowful?

ALERT

The day my cellphone buzzed an alert
we sat at lunch among startled diners,
the sound of emergency, desperate and chilling—
Pres. Trump announcing "I am the great I am"
in an unbidden text message,
playing at God
and crowing control like a mad rooster;

an hour later,
another message breaking silence:
days of this life brief for Sister Mary Zita,
an alert about pain, morphine, letting us know
she was holding on,
the white stars on her wool cap
fading into nowhere known

leaving us to choose:
answer an alert
of black feathered terror
or a twilight crossing
into the Also World,
hatred and love winking
like dual landing lights,

answer the near death
of a beloved nun
unlikely to be on the nightly news
or cruel tweets from a buffoon
poised to blow up the world:
heaven or hell
the final destination.

THE WORLD OVER-POPULATED WITH A.D.D.

Intractable groove of the brain
in bondage to illusions:
Self as Special, Entitled,
Popular, but never completing
The Work, going 'round and 'round,
a dervish trying to curry favor,
gypsy moth drawn to different flames
moment. by moment wanting a fix,
his fate more important than others
and wailing about his ignoble image
overlooked by more stable forms
that set fire to his expectations.

ENTRY IN JOURNAL ABOUT WARD, VETERAN'S HOSPITAL, PINEVILLE, LOUISIANA

"What religion are you?" The man who once worked on railroads had been waiting for a chance to taunt me with history.

"Episcopalian. Ordained deacon."

"Old Henry," he snorts.

"The Eighth," I finish for him. "But also Elizabeth I."

"And a whole lot of Catholics building the bridge over which they walked." He snorted again.

"And the Pope?"

"Well, who's at the top of your totem pole?"

"The Archbishop of Canterbury."

"Same thing. You got a new one several years ago. I keep up." He looked at me out of agonized eyes, moved the stump of one leg from under the covers.

"Yes, you do," I acknowledge. "But the Lord's always the same."

"Yeah," he answers. "But he did have two good legs. Can you say a Hail Mary for me?"

I nodded and pulled up the sheet, saying words that would release the wheelchair brake in his mind so he could envision walking down the hall.

Phantom limbs roamed the halls, unlikely companions leaving a pile of dirty linens, daring me to lie down and sleep, while so many in bed after bed, were caught in rotting skin. It was the hour of evening angst.

A crow cried his raucous message as I went out into daylight. The black dragon's message: You survived another night in the hospital. Pray that some day they will be exempt from bed sores, the smell of antiseptic and urine, and walk into the wellness of morning.

FIRST SIGNS

The first winter night on the mountain
rides in on a hard north wind;
moles scurry beneath the house
hearing giant acorns pinging
above their tunnels, thinking rain.

Our front yard wavers like corduroy,
hills throwing up dirt and earthworms
from a closed universe.
We watch from the kitchen window
feeling warmth drain away

when we see velvet bodies emerge
squealing as they ascend
the road leading upward,
winter becoming a pale moon
watching the late show.

ACKNOWLEDGEMENTS

To Darrell Bourque, whose closing to e-mail messages inspired the title for *All Love*, and for his support and friendship throughout 37 years;

To Karen Bourque, for the lovely lotus glass piece that provided the photograph for the cover of *All Love*, and for inspiring me many times;

To Vickie Sullivan, for forty years of inspiration, support, programming, and producing much of my work, particularly the volumes of poetry;

To Martin Romero, for his handsome design work on my books of poetry;

To "Kathy" Hamman, one of my best readers and supporters and for faithful friendship;

To Stuart Friebert for his endorsement and continued support;

To Gary and Susan Entsminger, editors and publishers of Pinyon Publishing, for constant support and friendship.

www.ingramcontent.com/pod-product-compliance
Lightning Source LLC
Chambersburg PA
CBHW051837040426
42447CB00006B/577